Young Boys and their Writing

Engaging young boys in the writing process

Written by
Jenni Clarke

Additional material and editing by
Sally Featherstone

Published 2009 by A & C Black Publishers Limited
36 Soho Square, London W1D 3QY
www.acblack.com

First published 2008 by Featherstone Education Limited

ISBN 978-1-9060-2970-8

Text © Jenni Clarke 2008
Cover design by Kerry Ingham

The Key Issues series is edited by Sally Featherstone

A CIP record for this publication is available from the British Library.

Printed in Malta by Gutenberg Press Ltd.

This book is produced using paper that is made from wood grown in
managed, sustainable forests. It is natural, renewable and recyclable.
The logging and manufacturing processes conform to the environmental
regulations of the country of origin.

To see our full range of titles
visit www.acblack.com

CONTENTS

Introduction

'Boys are not less able than girls, so perhaps we do need to look at our own attitudes, if we are to better understand why they are making less progress in the EYFS and beyond. The quality of our relationships with them, and the values we hold will impact on boys' ability to engage confidently in the learning process. Are we planning experiences for boys that build on their interests and value their strengths as active learners and problem solvers, or are we simply expecting them to be compliant, passive recipients of new skills and knowledge? Are we utilising boys' fascinations and learning preferences as starting points for our planning?'

Confident, capable and creative:
supporting boys' achievements; DCSF 2007

This quote from a recent DCSF guidance on supporting the achievements of boys, underpins our intentions for this book. It identifies not just the problem boys are having with the expectations they face in our settings and schools, but the relationships and attitudes of the adults who plan the environment for learning and the expectations for behaviour.

Most of the practitioners and teachers who work with the under sevens are women, who understand how girls learn, but may not understand that many boys learn very differently. Most girls have an innate ability to read faces, expressions and body language. They find it easier to sit still, they have a desire to meet our expectations, and they develop language and fine motor skills much earlier than most boys. This gives them a head start over boys in the sorts of activities expected by the education system, including the difficult skills of reading and writing.

Boys are NOT less clever than girls - but they are different! Their bodies are still in strong, physical, gross motor development mode during the early years of schooling, and their brains do develop more slowly, particularly in those areas that support fine motor skills.

Steve Biddulph in 'Raising Boys':

'At the age of six or seven, when children start serious schooling, boys are six to twelve months less developed mentally than girls. They are especially delayed in what is called 'fine motor coordination', which is the ability to use their fingers carefully and hold a pen or scissors. And since they are still in the stage of 'gross motor' development, they will be itching to move their large muscles around - so they will not be good at sitting still.'

We should all understand that asking boys to do something they are incapable of can result in destroying their self esteem for the rest of their school days, underlining that 'school is not for me!'.

For young children, making marks for a reason is a crucial stage in writing. If they see the purpose and enjoy the results of communicating on paper they will continue to do so as they develop handwriting skills and the ability to form conventional letter shapes.

However, there are many young children who believe that they cannot write because their writing does not look like writing in a book, like their parents' or like the teacher's. Such children often will not even try because in their minds they are going to fail - many of these children are boys.

As adults, we do not need to be able to read a child's writing to accept it, even if the child tells different people the words mean different things. The recognition of the difference between pictures and print is a significant step towards understanding reading and writing, and as long as the marks have meaning to the child, they should be recognised and rewarded as such by us. Many adults cannot read Chinese or Arabic characters but would still recognise them as communication in writing.

Research in many countries has highlighted that boys are not achieving the same standards in writing as girls, and that many boys also have a more negative attitude to writing. As early as 1998, government analysis in the UK, in a report titled 'Can do Better' noted:

> 'At Key Stage 1 (around 7 years), 21% of girls achieved Level 3 in the English tests, compared with 14% of boys.'

> 'Many boys write less than girls and are less enthusiastic and committed writers. On average they become competent later than girls, and are more likely to have problems as writers.'

> and

> 'A group of early years teachers observed that more girls than boys used the dedicated writing areas and for longer periods of time. The few boys who did use the writing table often remained standing, used the mark makers for a specific purpose such as putting their name on a model or making a sign for a road layout and then returned to a previous activity or moved on. Since members of staff used the writing table for routine tasks, it was likely that girls experienced more adult support and encouragement in writing.

> Can do Better, Raising Boys' Achievement in English; QCA 1998

This study seems to indicate that the children who need the support most, in fact often get least!

'From a young age boys choose to spend more time on activities which do not involve adults... In general, boys prefer active pursuits and may find it harder to acquire the more sedentary skills of reading and writing.'

'Can do Better' presented a number of case studies where teachers, some in Nurseries and Reception classes, had tried strategies to address these problems, and many had been successful.

However, the booklet was not widely used, and the introduction of the Foundation Stage guidance overtook its recommendations. In nearly a decade, little appears to have changed, and the government has now produced further guidance on raising the achievement of boys.

In 2007, a guidance document on supporting boys' achievements (Confident, capable and creative: supporting boys' achievements; DCSF) was produced to support the implementation of the Early Years Foundation Stage Curriculum (from birth to five). It amplified the previous report by noting that even at around five years of age:

'National data from the UK Foundation Stage Profile, 2004/2006, suggests that boys are achieving less well than girls across all areas of learning and that more girls are working securely within the early learning goals than boys.

Confident, capable and creative: supporting boys' achievements; DCSF 2007;

The achievement of boys is not just a UK concern. Educational establishments and governments in Australia, Canada, New Zealand and United States as well as the United Kingdom have been trying with varied success to address the issue over the past few years, and some of the initiatives and projects that have been successful in schools are discussed in the next chapter.

Girls out-perform boys in reading throughout the western world.

'More boys than girls acknowledged the frustrations of writing, mentioning problems with handwriting and punctuation.'

Cathie Holden; 2002

Is it any wonder that boys are 'switched off' when in this target obsessed time, they are consistently told they are not doing as well as girls.

Recent years have also seen a huge rise in the number of books for teachers and parents about gender, the differences between boys and girls, and how to help and support both. Parents have always known there is a difference, but new research into brain growth, the rise of feminism, and a culture of 'Girl Power' have all added to the pressure to succeed. Boys are beginning to be the victims of this, and boy behaviour where self esteem is low is now just as difficult for parents or society to cope with as the culture of the over-assertive girl.

Their fine motor development - the ability to string beads or print their names - lags behind girls' by about a year'.
Gabrielle Bauer
(2005)

Throughout this book you will find quotes from writers who are concerned to protect boys from early feelings of failure, while ensuring that girls still get the support they need. These writers include Steve Biddulph, Michael Gurian, Elizabeth Hartley Brewer, Vivienne Gussin Paley, Dan Kindlon and Michael Tompson, Lucinda Neall and William Pollack, just some of the adults who believe that we 'could do better' in our work with young boys.

'Because boys' brains are not suited, on average, for classrooms that emphasise reading, writing and complex word making, any culture that relies greatly on those techniques is set up for problems with a number of boys and young men.'
Michael Gurian; The Minds of Boys; 2005

and of course, throughout the western world we have just that culture.

As children move from the early years into statutory schooling, the situation only gets worse! When children become older they are being expected to produce writing in approximately 80% of lessons, something that often makes them feel a failure. This frontal attack on self-esteem or motivation can have a major effect, not just during school years, but for the rest of their lives. Many boys (and some girls) never get over this early attach when their self esteem is so vulnerable, and the activity becomes an obstacle throughout their lives:

'I'm no good at writing, Miss ... what's the point?' (11 year old boy)'

Fisher R; 2002

In his book 'Real Boys', William Pollack reports:

'Recent studies show that not only is boys' self esteem more fragile than that of girls and that boys' confidence as learners is impaired but also that boys are substantially more likely to endure disciplinary problems, be suspended from classes or actually drop out of school'

And in 'When Children Don't Learn', Diane McGuinness muses:

'In the early years, children concentrate on reading and writing, skills that largely favour girls. As a result, boys fill remedial reading classes, don't learn to spell, and are classified as dyslexic or learning-disabled four times as often as girls. Had these punitive categories existed earlier, they would have included Faraday, Edison and Einstein.'

This book attempts to address some of the issues related to boys and the writing process. We have chosen to narrow the focus to make it manageable for practitioners and teachers, and to ensure we give practical help and manageable ideas to adults and children in the Early Years.

About this book

Although the book is primarily aimed at inspiring boys to make meaningful marks and engage with the writing process, many of the practical ideas will appeal to girls too, negative feelings about writing are not exclusive to boys, just more frequent.

However, there are gender differences that do need to be taken into account. Developmentally girls tend to reach milestones earlier than boys, particularly in the area of language development, processing language, hearing and fine motor skills. This obviously makes writing more difficult for boys to achieve as they may not have the language structure to invent sentences or the physical ability to hold and control a mark-making implement.

This is one of the reasons so many boys do not enjoy writing and because of this they need more active enjoyable opportunities to use spoken language and play with mark making for a purpose. They need ample opportunities to use their whole bodies as they learn, to learn both indoors and outside, to have a real purpose to their activities, and to feel they are doing something worthwhile. Girls are noted as having the 'ability to manage boredom' and this enables them to sit and listen and to involve themselves in activities which have no apparent relevance to their interests.

The ideas included in this book and reasons behind the ideas will help to make the activities you present to early writers more varied, interesting, engaging and relevant to children's own worlds, and relevance is a key factor in remembering.

The activities section provides ideas for using play situations where it is natural and easy to include writing for a purpose, as well as hints for helping babies and children to develop the physical ability to hold, handle and control mark-making implements.

'With appropriate play situations to reveal literacy behaviour, children do demonstrate a commitment to writing, inquisitiveness about writing, and knowledge about writing.'

Nigel Hall and Anne Robinson; 2003

What has worked
in settings and schools?

Projects, initiatives and strategies to improve boys' literacy, and writing in particular, have been many and varied, and have been implemented in schools all over the world. Some of the strategies that have been successful in motivating boys to have a go and get interested in writing are:

Using film, pictures and other visual stimuli to inspire writing

In a reception class in England; traditional tales were a focus in the medium term plan. The teacher decided to use video clips from Peter Pan, with an aim of making individual books with the children.

The adults selected stills from the film and pictures from the book to use as prompts for discussion and drawing. The children watched short clips from the film, and listened to short extracts read from the book.

The children were then given plenty of time to talk, to re-enact the story, discussing characters and scenes before doing any writing. They were inspired by the familiar story, and they used a much wider range of vocabulary than in previous sessions.

In a Year One class (5 to 6 year olds) a teacher used video clips from Pocahontas, the children were given time for discussion and analysis, and when it came to writing they were keen to start. Inspired by the images and music, many of the boys wrote more than ever before and a few even stopped to ask for spellings.

> 'The children were proud of their finished pieces of work and I am sure it gave them the incentive to try again on the next piece.'   Primary National Strategy; 2004

The teacher learned that if the written outcome is given time, is built up over weeks then the children will produce writing of much better quality.

> 'I find using different types of visual or interactive texts such as film/DVD can engage even the most un-motivated young writers. Writing can become a much more enjoyable experience when text and image work together. They become absorbed in it and don't want to stop!'   Foundation Stage Practitioner; 2005

Using ICT to inspire writing

Nine schools in Kent, with interactive whiteboards and teachers confident in using ICT used these to support boys' writing. They used a software package to teach and inspire the children, and found

 that, using the program helped boys to show more motivation, contribute more to lessons, and participate more in discussion. Older children were asked their opinions -

'It helps me to learn and understand things more easily.'
'It helps me to learn more because, instead of the teacher telling me and I don't get it, I can see it for myself.'
'I can click a paragraph and it will speak it out for you.'
'It makes hard lessons fun to do in class and helps you (rather) than just writing work with no help.'

Boyz 2 Rite; 2004

Both these projects showed that boys are more motivated if the material to inspire writing is fun, familiar and visual. They also write better if they have time to talk and discuss ideas, building up the vocabulary before using it in writing. Often children are asked to write before they have had time to formulate ideas, test their ideas on their peer group, think about changes and impact of words, decide beginnings, endings, journeys in the middle, discuss and try out their characters. Once all this is secure, then the physical aspect of writing is not distracting from the quality of the content. **What** is going to be written does not need to dominate **how** it is written.

Time for talk before writing

Teacher's TV (2007) in England discussed the issue of talk. Boys generally talk later then girls and develop linguistic skills later, so they need more time to talk and discuss before writing, this enables them to develop ideas and a wider range of vocabulary. They need time to organise their ideas once their creative thoughts begin to flow.

The DfES support 'Talk for Writing', and produced a leaflet in 2005 to encourage teachers to plan more time for talk before writing. They stress that it is most effective in encouraging all children to write well when it has been carefully planned and structured.

An example from the leaflet says:

> 'Children in the Foundation Stage visited a farm park. One of the keepers showed the children around the farm and told them about the animals that they saw. They were able to stroke and feed some of them. Back in the setting, the children talked about what they had seen and done and recalled the information that they had been told. They worked together on a group recount of their day out, which they tape recorded and played to parents and carers.'

> 'I find that the writing improves in my class when we have talked about it because this helps children with the content of what is to be written. It allows them to rehearse the structure and the sequence of the writing and guides how the text should sound - its style and voice. It also encourages my children to generate and rehearse appropriate language as they work collaboratively to plan, draft and improve their writing.'   Y1 teacher; 2005

Linked with this is time for talk during writing and time for talk after writing, boys often need frequent and constructive feedback to enable them to continue to value and enjoy their writing.

> 'I like it when the teacher talks to me on my own... she tells me how I'm doing and helps me.'   Charlie, aged 5; 2005

The Key Principles of 'Talk for Writing' are:

- Children learning English as an additional language benefit from orally rehearsing writing;
- Children need to activate knowledge of what they are going to write about. This can be done in a first or additional language;
- Children need to experience language being used in order to be able to use it effectively themselves;
- Talk for writing can be used across the curriculum;
- Boys and girls may communicate in different ways. We can make the most of the differences by planning a variety of different groups, pairings and seating arrangements;
- The collaborative skills developed through talk for writing can be used in social as well as academic situations;
- Drama is a successful tool to stimulate writing at all ages;
- Talk for writing is most effective when it is a carefully planned, thoroughly prepared, part of learning;
- The teacher/practitioner's own talk can be a powerful way of demonstrating talk for writing;
- Signing and alternative means of communication should be used where appropriate.

Boys need active learning

Peter West , Head of the Research Group on Men and Families, University of Western Sydney, Australia (*What is the Matter with Boys?* 2002) carried out and collated information about boys and school achievement.

One of the outcomes was the boys' ability to enjoy learning which was hands on, active, and exploratory in nature. When teaching included real objects, going out on visits, acting out, discussions and other active learning, the boys' attention and achievement increased.

Research in Australia also highlights how important active learning is for children in general and boys in particular. Teaching

'Boys need and want to move, and they learn by doing'.

The Getting it Right Enquiry; 2002

that allows movement, hands on, physical involvement - such as drama in literacy - will increase boy's attitudes and achievement.

Brain research also tells us that movement, engagement and hands on activities are keys to high quality brain activity.

Using drama to inspire writing

A group of schools in England were involved in improving boys writing through drama. The idea was to use practical drama activities linked to writing frames in order to motivate boys to write.

The drama activities enabled the boys to think through what they could write, what the characters might be, and writing frames gave them a structure to support the organisation of the writing.

'The boys' attitude and motivation to produce good quality writing increased!'

Pippa Dorran; 2003

Another school used drama to increase the creative content of writing rather than concentrating on the grammar. They also used partner work which involved talking, discussing and analysing their ideas. The result was increased motivation and better quality and quantity of written work.

In Australia children are:

> 'Wearing the latest weapon in the battle to improve literacy amongst boys.'
>
> Australian Broadcasting Corporation; 2004

They are wearing red velvet capes printed with the words 'Star Writer' on the back. This seems to be encouraging the boys to have a go at writing as they wish to be like a super hero!! They can act like a Star Writer and feel good about themselves at the same time.

Writing for a purpose

Writing for a real purpose, knowing that there is a reason for writing, is vitally important to all young children, and to boys in particular, especially when they are being asked to do something they may find difficult. If children are given enough experiences of writing for a relevant purpose at an early stage, then writing just becomes a natural part of their play and learning.

> 'Children are more likely to write as part of purposeful play.'
>
> Curriculum Guidance for the Foundation Stage; 2000

The DfES leaflet Improving Boys' Writing: Purpose and Audience, stresses the importance for boys of having a purpose in mind. If they have to write, then they want to know that it has a use. 'Real' writing experiences for a real audience will give boys something to achieve, they do not want to spend time and energy on something just because the teacher wants it.

> 'I find that the boys in my class are more enthusiastic in their writing if each task has a very clear purpose.'
>
> Jane, Year 5 teacher; 2005

If children are to be motivated to use skills they find difficult, they must have an interest in the activity. It is the responsibility of practitioners and teachers to observe and talk with the children in their groups, so that they can find out what 'switches individuals on' to using writing for real purposes.

It is interesting to note that practitioners and teachers are now being advised to incorporate these activities, successful with older children, into the programme for younger children. Young children are natural learners and communicators, and this natural tendency can be nurtured and used to support the use of writing through practical experiences.

Many of the practical ideas in this book incorporate these strategies as well as the essential elements of enjoyment, play, creativity and ownership of learning.

The act of writing

All adults know that the act of writing is a very complicated skill, but, once we have learned how to do it, it is easy to forget just what is involved.

There are two aspects to the act of writing -

- the mental aspect: the ideas, structure, linguistic knowledge, organisational skills and concentration

and

- the physical aspect: fine motor skills, gross motor skills, hand-eye coordination, ability to be still and control the muscles of the body.

The mental aspect is acquired through talking, listening to stories, reading, looking at pictures,

playing with stories and words and experience of living with others. Without a language structure, a wide vocabulary and motivating experiences, a child cannot be expected to write, for what would they write about?

The physical aspect demands control of many muscles, not just those which control fingers and hands. Trunk, shoulder and upper arm muscles, back and bottom muscles to control sitting, and coordinated eye muscles all need to be developed, controlled and available for writing.

Stimulating the brain and body to write

Remember that if children are going to learn, all their language experiences should be enjoyable. If a story or picture is accompanied by a barrage of questions, it becomes a test of knowledge and is not a pleasurable experience for child or adult.

From the earliest age, when babies are just learning to talk, they love to name and label things in the world, so they can make sense of them. They need to hear the correct names as well as being encouraged to use their own names for an object. We all know the technique of responding to a child saying 'fine gingin' by replying, 'yes, it is a fire engine' - giving encouragement and modelling at the same time.

Too many questions or corrections can also make some children, especially some boys, feel inadequate, and the damage to self esteem in language can begin. Be aware that questions, particularly closed questions, and specially questions in front of their peers can be very stressful for young children.

So try to make your questions:
- relevant to the child (will they be interested in the question?)
- clear and easily understood (do they know what you mean?)
- open (do you expect and recognise more than a 'yes/no' answer?)
- positively posed (is your attitude sufficiently non-confrontational?)
- accepting of differing responses (do you encourage a range of responses?).

Are we planning experiences for boys that build on their interests and value their strengths as active learners and problem solvers, or are we simply expecting them to be compliant, passive recipients of new skills and knowledge?

Confident, capable and creative:
supporting boys' achievements; DCSF; 2007

Developing the linguistic structures of learning to write (ideas, linguistic knowledge, organisational skills and concentration)

Here are some essential experiences for babies and young children which will prepare them for thinking, responding and communicating. Of course, some children will already have had these experiences in supportive and communicating homes, but others may not, and we do have some emerging evidence that many children are not experiencing language rich environments at home.

Children at home and at school should:

- hear plenty of songs and rhymes, including nursery rhymes and jingles;
- join in with songs and rhymes;
- look at pictures of rhymes and songs while singing and chanting them;
- listen to stories, with and without pictures or a book;
- make up their own stories about familiar events and things that happen;
- talk about what they do, what they have done, what they are going to do.

Adults (parents, carers, practitioners) at home and in settings should:

- talk to babies and toddlers, involving them in what is happening around, naming and categorising objects, events and pictures;
- watch carefully for children's responses (verbal and non-verbal), and respond in turn;
- involve babies and young children in making up their own stories, storytelling is a vital preparation and accompaniment to writing;
- talk about everyday happenings, such as food (how it tastes, feels or looks); events (walks, visits, visitors); things they see, feel, touch (birds in the trees, planes and cars, shops, pebbles and shells, weather etc.), modelling the use of language and new vocabulary;
- provide shared sensory experiences and active learning, with adults using a wide range of vocabulary to describe what is experienced;
- look at pictures and photos, talk about what can be seen, comment on what is happening, and encourage children to join in.

Older children need to continue all the earlier experiences, reinforcing their language and developing new skills as they move from using single words and sounds, to word clusters and then sentences. Rhyme continues to be an essential part of language learning, and the rhymes and songs children hear, say and learn are essential to future reading and to writing and spelling.

Children at home and at school should:

- continue to play with rhymes and sounds, making up new endings and new words to familiar rhymes - rhyming should be fun, and the rhyming words don't have to make sense!
- continue to create their own stories, sometimes using an adult as a 'scribe', and using these stories for dramatisation, reading at story time, collected in a special book, read out and acted by the children, ensuring that these stories are valued;
- act out rhymes, songs, stories and poems - this is a great way to ensure that boys are on task and learning new vocabulary;
- be encouraged to use descriptive words at snack time, food is a great motivator.

Remember that many boys are likely to need more encouragement to talk and to develop their vocabulary than most girls.

Adults (parents, carers, practitioners) in settings should:

- ensure that the environment has plenty of real reasons for looking at or 'reading' words and signs, such as labels alongside pictures, captions with pictures, signs for play indoors and out, information about the day;
- listen as well as talk, answer questions as well as ask them;
- model being a reader and a writer as well as being a talker;
- remember that talk encourages talk.

'Before, we had never acted out these stories (dictated by children). We had dramatised every other kind of printed word - fairly tales, story books, poems, songs - but it had always seemed enough just to write the children's words. Obviously it was not; the words did not sufficiently represent the action, which needed to be shared.

Wally's Stories; Vivian Gussin Paley

Developing the physical skills of learning to write: (fine and gross motor skills, hand-eye coordination, the ability to be still, control the muscles of the body)

The physical aspect of writing is developed through running, climbing, rolling, manipulating materials, sensory experiences and playing with a wide variety of toys and equipment. Without a well developed muscle structure, and a knowledge and experience of using both fine and gross motor movements a child cannot be expected to begin to make controlled and meaningful marks.

Many people think of writing as simply a fine motor skill, but it also involves the larger muscles in the shoulders, arms and back. Fine motor skills use the small muscles in the hand for precise movements and develop during childhood, however these can only develop when there is control of the larger muscles.

Muscle control generally develops from the top of the body downwards and from the centre outwards, which means that the fingers are one of the last muscles a child will have good control over. Development of the shoulders and upper arms allows more control over the hand and fingers, and children need good control of the centre of the body and the hips to be comfortable with sitting. Children also need kinesthetic awareness - to be able to feel where and how the shoulder, arm and hand move, so they need to develop gross motor control alongside fine motor control.

Gross motor movements also encourage the development of pathways between the left and right hemispheres of the brain, essential for coordinating both eyes, both ears and both hands.

To ensure that the art of writing is physically easier for young boys make sure they get plenty of opportunities to do what they like doing best! Running, swinging, playing ball, climbing, pushing and pulling toys, digging etc. All these activities are preparing their bodies for writing, developing the core, and fine motor muscles and links in the brain.

'Many boys, however, can be months, sometimes years, behind in the development stakes. The requirement to sit still, listen for individual sounds in language, relate these sounds to abstract symbols, and then manipulate a pencil to draw the symbols is beyond their capacity. They just aren't ready for it.'

Sue Palmer ; 2002

'When children's physical and emotional needs are met they are more ready to take advantage of the play and learning opportunities on offer.'   EYFS; 2007

Developing gross motor skills in babies and children

Here are some essential experiences for babies and young children which will help to develop gross motor skills. Of course, some children will already have had these experiences in active and engaging homes.

Babies and young children at home and in settings and schools should have:

- space for rolling, stretching, crawling and exploring indoors and outdoors;
- cushions, tunnels, boxes, soft blocks for climbing over, under and through;
- balls, ribbons, textured material, squeaky toys hanging on elastic so that they move when touched or pulled; or spring up when released;
- trays or paddling pools with water, bubbles, cornflour and water to encourage stirring, mixing, feeling;
- walls, floor spaces, objects of different textures to encourage reaching, moving, feeling;
- paint or easy-to-hold mark making materials, large sheets of paper or material, for mark making on a large scale;
- large and small mirrors at low levels, so they can see themselves moving;
- collections of interesting objects to be handled, squeezed, pulled, rolled;
- push-along equipment to encourage upper arm strength;
- balls, bean bags, scarves, ribbons, ribbon sticks, Koosh balls for throwing, waving, rolling, catching, pushing or kicking.

Adults (parents, carers, practitioners) at home and in settings should:

- ensure that children have space, indoors and outside, for moving and playing;
- provide play out of doors every day;
- ensure they provide a wide range of physical and sensory experiences.

Older children at home and in schools should continue to experience all the opportunities offered to younger children, plus:

- painting with water and paint, using large brushes on big surfaces, paper, fabric, paving;
- painting or using big chalks on walls, fences, wall mounted blackboards, long rolls of paper, sheets;
- playing with ribbons, football scarves, flags, saris, simple kites, parachute material in a large space outdoors in still and windy weather;
- crawling through tunnels, under and through PE equipment, under blankets;
- playing parachute games;
- pulling and moving with large pieces of lycra material;
- pushing, driving and wheeling wheelbarrows, tractors and other ride-on toys;
- digging in the garden - not for gardening, but just digging!

Adults (parents, carers, practitioners) at home and in settings should:

- provide play out of doors every day;
- a wide range of physical and sensory experiences;
- provide space to move indoors and outdoors;
- include activities that involve hopping, running, balancing or skipping - these are helpful as general gross motor co-ordination, laying the groundwork for smooth, fine muscle control;
- offer activities that involve using both hands - sewing, threading, construction, sand, water, dough etc.
- include activities where children are using two tools, one in each hand - painting or drawing with two brushes, two crayons, two chalks;
- offer hand sprayers with water or dilute food colouring for spray painting;
- make sure children have a wide range of equipment to use in sand, water, construction;
- collect a wide range of recycled materials for building, constructing and play out of doors.

Developing fine motor skills in babies and children

Here are some essential experiences for babies and young children which will help to develop fine motor skills. Of course, some children will already have had these experiences in active and engaging homes.

Babies and young children at home and in settings and schools should be:

- exploring and feeling paint, flour, cornflour and water, soap, sand, dry rice in trays;
- exploring and playing with a variety of mark making implements in sand, rice, cornflour and water;
- finger painting;
- making marks on different surfaces with a variety of materials (The Little Book of Mark Making has lots of ideas);
- exploring and feeling small textured bags filled with sand, rice, dried beans of different sizes, dried seeds of different sizes;
- playing with soft toys of different textures;
- manipulating different coloured and scented dough or clay.

Adults (parents, carers, practitioners) at home and in settings should:

- massage children's fingers and hands with gentle creams to ensure that muscles are relaxed as they grow;
- encourage children to play with dough and pastry - cooking and dough play should be a regular activity;
- provide plenty of opportunities to explore holes, posting boxes, easy threading, inset jigsaws, simple construction toys, dolls and soft toys with clothes; purses, bags, boxes and baskets to fill and empty; simple pegs and pegboards etc.

Older children at home, and in settings and schools should have further experience of all the previously listed activities plus:

- screwing up paper to make balls to throw or flick into a box or bucket;
- table football with a small ball and flicking fingers;
- posting objects such as coins, keys, toys, parcels, letters, numbers into slots and holes;
- using pegs on a line or box to make patterns, peg up clothes, soft toys, pictures or instructions;
- using pegs and other joining materials such as tape, cable ties, clips to fix clothing and role play fabrics, or to make dens and shelters;
- playing with keys and locks;
- threading buttons, beads, keys, dry pasta;
- learning to use fastenings on clothing and shoes (buttons, zips, laces, Velcro, hooks etc);
- using simple tools such as hammers and screwdrivers;
- tying knots in wool and string;
- throwing and catching smaller objects;
- building with small construction equipment and large recycled materials such as guttering, tyres, planks;
- gardening, using small size tools.

Adults (parents, carers, practitioners) at home and in settings should:

- encourage children to be as independent as possible in dressing and undressing themselves;
- model, teach and support the safe and independent use of tools and cutlery;
- encourage and praise perseverance in learning the complex movements of fine motor control.

Valuing Writing

'Early Years Foundation Stage; Effective Practice - Practitioners who monitor all children's progress regularly through discussing documentation and their learning diaries, sharing these with the child and parents and planning next steps that will engage and motivate them to continue to be interested and excited to learn.'

Confident, capable and creative: supporting boys' achievements; DCSF; 2007

Children, and many boys in particular, like to have a reason for doing things, and this applies to writing too! If they spend time and effort producing a piece of writing then it needs to be useful to them, and valued by you, even if you can't read it without their help. We want all children to see writing as something they can do for fun, for different reasons and for different people.

Some of the ways you can do this are:

Valuing writing by displaying it

This does not mean only displaying writing that is in conventional marks that can be read, but displaying and using writing that comes in a variety of forms, readable without the child, or not. It is communication, not readability that is important.

- Ensure that displays are updated regularly, talked about, used.
- Involve children in putting up the display so that they know it is there and what it is about.
- Change displays frequently enough to stimulate comment, but long enough to really value their content. Some displays are by nature transient and may only stay for a day, others will provide a discussion focus for weeks - but take them down when children (or you) stop noticing them.
- Spend time and effort presenting children's writing carefully and imaginatively, but don't be tempted to make the presentation so exciting that the writing is lost or under-valued.
- Offer display space at child height so children can display items of importance to them.

- **Have a message board** where children, adults and visitors can stick up messages to each other, the adults can put up messages too, and these messages can be read out to a child, a small group or all the children. Adults need to be seen to be writing messages to each other too, reading them and responding. Have name cards near the board for the children to use, so it is easy to see who the message is for. Post boxes are great too!

- Within the role play area have a display space for examples of completed forms, letters, notices, signs and other writing. Make sure the adults use this space, writing themselves, and commenting on the writing displayed.

- Send some letters or cards to the group and see what the response is - you could ask for help or information, invite the children to join an event, or pose a problem to be solved.

- Where creative work is displayed, let the children write their own names and descriptions, and mount these as carefully as you would in an exhibition.

- In the construction area have a board for displaying plans, ideas, drawings of finished objects, leaflets etc. Include adult examples too, displaying all pieces of writing with the same care and attention.

- Display writing and mark making that has been created during outdoor play near the outside door to give children ideas and also to demonstrate that their writing could be displayed too. Make laminated outdoor notices and signs, and even a weatherproof notice board, covered with heavy plastic or perspex.

- Bound, zig-zag, folded and shaped books are a great way of displaying children's writing. Hang them up or put them on shelving, in your book corner. It could be a book of police crime reports, car number plates, a list of names and portraits, a scrapbook or the re-telling of a favourite story - just like adults, children love to be published.

- Capture and display spontaneous writing done during play - if children are using white boards then try to photocopy some before they are wiped. You may need to be quick!

- Have a 'We are all writers' space, where any writing can be displayed under headings such as fiction/stories, fact and poems. Involve adults too.

- Remember that writing goes hand in hand with reading, so there should be plenty of examples of different types of writing displayed around the room for real reasons too - labels, signs, reminders, helpful hints, forms in specific areas, safety rules, and a board for messages such as 'James is going home with Matthew today' or 'The plants need watering on Wednesday'. Children need to get used to different sorts of print and shapes of letters, so you could collect some different looking versions of letters from magazines, adverts and junk mail.

Valuing writing by talking about it and modelling it

Talking about writing, both the process and the product is vital. Most practitioners who work in the early years are very comfortable about talking about the finished product of children's mark making and writing - but some are less comfortable with talking about how to start and sustain writing. Everyone (children included) needs time to think about the 'w's of writing:

- what they want to say - what is the writing going to contain,

  what form it will take - will it be a notice? a letter? a list? a labelled diagram? a story? a sign?

  and what will they use - paper? card? chalk? whiteboard? mud?

- where and how they are going to do it - indoors? out of doors? lying down? standing up?

- when they will do it - now? tomorrow? 'later'?

- why it is important to them to write - the purpose of the writing - self initiated? adult directed? an imperative?

- and who they will involve as they plan and think about the activity - adults? other children? - and in what role - as scribe? collaborator? co-writer?

Model talking through the writing process, for example:

> 'I'm going to write a notice to make sure no one bangs their head as they go in our cave. I need it to be bright, so they'll notice it. What do I need?
>
> I think I'll use yellow paper and a big black pen. OK, now if I write DANGER in big letters that might work. Then MIND YOUR HEAD so everyone knows what the danger is.
>
> I need to write the word DANGER, D-A-N-G-E-R that looks right, ...'

This 'thinking aloud' helps children to get an idea of the thought processes that occur when writing. If you make 'thinking aloud' an accepted and valued process in your setting or school, it also makes it easier to understand how a child is approaching the task of writing. Thinking about thinking (metacognition) is a skill that we all need to practice, and children need to get used to the language of this process.

> 'I do not ask the children to stop thinking about play. Our contract reads more like this: if you will keep trying to explain yourselves I will keep showing you how to think about the problems you need to solve.'
>
> Vivian Gussin Paley; Wally's Stories

Model asking for help and approval, and support a climate where it is OK to ask for help, ideas or comments on the writing process as well as on the end product. Adults can ask children for help, ideas or approval, children can ask other children or adults, and in a culture of cooperation not competition, everyone is willing to help.

An adult might say to children playing near them -

> 'What do you think? It says DANGER - MIND YOUR HEAD'. Is it clear enough? Does it need a picture? What should I draw? Where shall we put it?'

A child might say to an adult -

> 'Can you write my story for me? Then you can read it while we play it.'

A child might say to another child -

> 'I need you to help me make this card. It's for my new baby - how d'ya write "baby bruzzer"?'

And anyone might say to anyone else -

> 'I really like your book about Superman.' or 'Do you like my writing?' or 'Is this the way you ...?'

Model listening to children and adults as they talk about writing, for example:

- **If you ask for opinions** about your writing, you must be ready to listen carefully to comments and make changes. Reading it out to the children will encourage them to do the same with their writing. It doesn't matter that they can't read your writing, or that you can't read theirs, you know what you have written and they know what they have written. What you are doing is sharing the writing process.

- With individuals and small groups of children, look at some of the different types of writing around your room. Share positive comments about writing, encourage the children to praise each others' efforts, as peer approval is very important to everyone.

- Model constructive words for praise, avoiding empty or general statements such as 'That's nice.' Try to be clear about why you like the child's efforts -

  'I like the way you used long and short lines',

  'I can see the letter from your name.'

  'You have drawn these circles really carefully.'

  'How did you make this envelope for your letter?'

This will help the children to look at their own and other children's writing more carefully, and will signpost them towards the sorts of things to say in feedback.

- Respond to writing in the role play area, small world scenarios and outdoor boxes by showing that you have been listening to child-initiated play:

'In schools, when literacy resources are made available to playing children, they become a vital and sometimes critical part of the play'.

Nigel Hall & Anne Robinson

'I can see that Simon has had an adventure today - just look at all the maps and discoveries he has made.'

'Lots of people have ordered pizzas today, I can see all these messages in the book. You must have been very busy.'

'I was watching Michael and Hari writing with water on the wall outside. They were making adverts for the Spiderman film. I took this photo of them writing. Do you want to see them?'

Model writing by acting as a scribe:

- For many children, specially boys, having the offer of a scribe is a real lifeline in the concentrated and time consuming task of writing things down.
  This will help the children to look at their own and other children's writing more carefully, and will signpost them towards the sorts of things to say in feedback.
- Read some of Vivian Gussin Paley's books about how she scribes children's writing so they can play out their stories while she acts as narrator - try 'Wally's Stories' or 'Boys and Girls; Superheroes in the Doll Corner'

'The first time I asked Wally if he wanted to write a story he looked surprised. 'You didn't teach me to write yet,' he said.
'You just tell me the story, Wally. I'll write the words.'   Vivian Gussin Paley; Wally's Stories

Value writing by using it for activities:

- Act out stories, rhymes and poems, indoors and outside;
- Read and re-enact scenarios on fire report forms etc. so children realise their writing is taken seriously and can be used by other children.
- Sometimes post the letters that children write and engineer a reply from a friend or colleague. Or write real letters to real people - they will almost always reply!
- Send the thank you letters and pictures children write to visitors, then ask the visitor to reply, explaining how important it is for the children to get a response.
- Have a wise owl toy next to a tree letter box, and encourage the children to write questions down (about a topic or focus of interest, or about anything they choose), and put their name on it. During the day, an adult can ask some of the children to read their questions, the owl can tell the adult the answer in owl language, or suggest where the answer may be found.
- Encourage the children to write invitations to people they would like to meet. Their letters can be posted along with the adult's version, valued as just as important and worth reading.

Value writing through partnership with parents:

- Talk to parents and carers about the development of writing, and the importance of valuing all attempts, however small. Explain the importance of modelling being a writer, and that writing notes, lists and reminders, filling in forms, sending cards and even emailing are important ways to communicate information. Children, especially boys, need to see adults writing!

> Work closely with parents and families, developing mutual understanding of how boys and girls play and the importance of building on children's interests;
> **EYFS**

- Try a special board of photos, a video or a photo book that illustrates the stages of writing, with explanations of each stage. Make sure the value of praise is emphasised. Give the parents ideas of how to ask their child what something they have written means, such as ' I would love you to read the letter to me.' Make a leaflet of ideas for stimulating writing at home - you could:

- have a little box of scrap paper and pencils available in the kitchen for writing lists and notes;
- keep forms, envelopes, catalogues and junk mail for making letters and cards, form filling, scrap booking;
- give your child old diaries, appointment books, address books etc. for writing and drawing;
- make lists together;
- ask your child to write you reminders of something you need to remember to do or buy;
- make cards and scrap books together;
- sometimes send a letter or postcard to your child;
- let your child see you writing - even if it's only a shopping list;
- praise every attempt at writing, even if they have to read it to you!

'EYFS Principle: Children learn to be strong and independent from a base of loving and secure relationships with parents and/or a key person.'

Confident, capable and creative: supporting boys' achievements; DCSF 2007

Practical ideas and strategies
for enhancing your provision

Introduction and Context

It is difficult to separate reading and writing development as they occur together as a child is learning. The ideas in this chapter do concentrate on the writing aspect, but it is important to bear in mind that if children are going to be inspired to write, they need to see examples of both writers and writing. The environment needs to be a language and writing rich one, where reading and writing are part of everyday life and have a purpose rather than being a series of empty exercises.

Writing needs to be fun, practical, purposeful and recognised by the children as an integral part of their play. In play situations writing can reflect the real world, where it:

> is personal;
> has a consequence;
> is for a wide range of audiences;
> is often collaborative and social.

Using writing to communicate as part of a practical experience ensures that it is embedded in purposeful play and results from a real desire to write.

'Children are more likely to write as part of purposeful play.'

Curriculum Guidance for the Foundation Stage; 2000

'With appropriate play situations to reveal literacy behaviour, children do demonstrate a commitment to writing, inquisitiveness about writing, and knowledge about writing.'

Nigel Hall and Anne Robinson; 2003

A variety of audiences

Audiences are vital for young writers, and these should be as varied as possible. This range should include:

- friends;
- family members;
- adults in school;
- visitors;
- role play characters;
- story characters;
- puppets and soft toys.

Try to make communication with these audiences as real as possible by providing:

- a post box, with collections and deliveries;
- a notice board at child height where messages can be left;
- forms, envelopes, post-it notes, cards and writing paper in different colours, sizes and shapes for messages;
- pens (ball points, fine felt pens), staplers, tape and hole punches;
- clip boards and white boards for easy writing;
- access to word processing, printers, and perhaps email and fax;
- and - most important - a reply system that gives prompt and relevant feedback!
- and perhaps real replies through the post, delivered by the real postman!

Using different forms of technology

Boys are generally attracted to technology and this interest can be utilised in play situations. Using a telephone, writing down messages, appointment times. Digital camcorders are great for talk before writing, acting out and thinking through stories before anything is put onto paper. Digital cameras are inspiring because of the immediate feedback they give as well as the opportunities for making captions and labels. Dictaphones or tape recorders are wonderful for sharing ideas on a theme, for organising ideas before writing, for exploring story language and flow of thought. Computers are so invaluable for creating stories, pictures, captions, factual information books, photo books, presentations, or poems with recorded speech or music.

When you plan and organise role play situations, think about the technology that would naturally be available in that situation:

- a real or cardboard box TV in a home corner;
- a telephone and computer in a fire station;
- a computer and printer for a travel agent;
- an electronic till and calculator in a shop or Post Office;
- a dictaphone in an office;
- a mobile phone in a builder's yard;
- a camera for an interior decorator.

Adding paper, pens, magazines, forms, leaflets, notebooks, diaries, calendars, catalogues, photo books, will all stimulate mark making and writing in role.

Offer a challenge

Older children, and boys in particular like a challenge, it motivates them to stay on task and achieve more. There are challenge ideas for older children in the following chapters. Challenges can be verbal, but can be more effective on specially designed cards that the children can see. Any challenge attempted needs to be reviewed and discussed, to acknowledge successes and manage the difficulties and disappointments. If challenges are seen as valued and important more children will choose to attempt them. They may end up writing their own challenge cards for each other and even for adults, so be prepared to take up challenges too!

Movement

Movement is important as it triggers memory, so make sure there is plenty of opportunity for all children to move as they talk and write. Writing does not have to be done sitting at a table. Many boys (and some girls), specially at younger ages, need more space to spread out and do their work, and they may feel more comfortable kneeling, standing or lying down.

'The best thing schools can do is allow more movement and become more tolerant to sound. We tend to want our children quiet and seated at their desks. This is not the best situation for boys, whose brains learn better when they have frequent opportunities to move around.'

Kathy Stevens; 2006

Writing can happen anywhere

Out of doors is a fantastic place for writing - most young boys will prefer to be playing and learning outside. There is generally more space, and the opportunity to make more noise without disturbing others. If the majority of the boys in your care prefer to be outside, it is important they don't see writing just as an indoor, sitting at a table 'be quiet' activity.

Writing is more than a tabletop, serious, quiet, often teacher directed activity. Writing is a hugely enjoyable way of communicating thoughts, feelings, ideas, jokes, greetings, stories, and for expressing the imagination.

Remember the influential role adults can play in suggesting and modelling these practical ideas. Children need to see writing modelled in different situations, for different reasons and for different audiences. Adults need to get into role and play alongside, so the children understand the important place writing has in their play.

For example, you could work with a small group of children to put together an outside writing box, discussing what they choose to put in it, what it may be used for, and how the writing may occur during play. These children can introduce the box to others - the best way of learning is by teaching someone else!

The practical ideas are starting points for you to try, expand, adapt and experiment with. Make sure the activities you suggest or initiate link with the children's current interests, or are adapted accordingly. Playing alongside the children as you introduce the ideas will make it more engaging for them and will give you a better understanding of their interests and links with future activities. Writing for fun and enjoyment should be a priority for young children, older children and adults.

Writing everywhere!

A rich and varied environment supports children's learning and development. It gives them the confidence to explore and learn in safe, yet challenging, indoor and outdoor spaces.

Early Years Foundation Stage; DCSF; 2007

Many learning areas in your setting or classroom can be enhanced by including incidental writing opportunities, but some areas are more appealing to boys, so here are some ideas for these areas. Before making any changes, take time to observe the children in each of the learning areas to discover which ones the boys prefer, and gradually add writing opportunities to these areas. Remember that you can switch boys off activities if you make the writing too central - just offer the materials and ideas as incidentals or suggestions, and make sure the writing is for a real purpose!

Children also need your permission and model to know that materials from one area can be taken and used in another, to enhance or extend the play there. Here are some simple ideas for portable equipment:

- ✎. Small baskets with writing equipment such as pens, paper and little pads or books, diaries, appointment books;

- ✎. Backpacks with lots of pockets filled with writing equipment;

- ✎. Writing belts with pencils and other mark makers attached or in little pockets and loops;

- ✎. Small trolleys, such as vegetable baskets that can be easily wheeled outside or to another area of the room;

- ✎. 'Customised' writing objects - simple booklets with themed rubber stamps, magazines and other junk mail to cut and stick themed pictures on stories and books, superhero or TV character writing pads, pencils and pens to support current interests;

- ✎. Post-it pads, small offcuts of paper for lists and notes, pens on elastic or coiled tethers.

Ensure the resources are:

- ✏. attractive;
- ✏. in good condition;
- ✏. regularly topped up and replaced;
- ✏. in easily portable containers;
- ✏. of sufficient quantity, but not so much as to outface the children - several smaller containers are much easier to manage.

In your construction area

This area of an early years setting is usually full of boys. Construction is a highly creative activity, but at the same time involves deconstruction, which also appeals to boys' fascination with taking things apart.

Younger children need plenty of opportunities to see others using mark making as communication, and to be encouraged to make labels and pictures of their designs and constructions. Your example and model is essential here, using the resources and talking about what you are doing as you play alongside.

Some **resources** you could include:

- ✎. Hard hats and tabards, **with badges**;

- ✎. **Plenty of** recycled and creative materials;

- ✎. Photos and books **about construction sites, bridges, roads, buildings, towers and tunnels;**

- ✎. Vehicles **such as barrows and trucks;**

- ✎. Clipboards, forms, notepads, Post-it notes, labels;

- ✎. Plans, architectural drawings **and notes, designs;**

- ✎. Health and safety signs **and posters;**

- ✎. A desk and pinboard **for display.**

Reasons for writing:

- ✎. Signing in to the site;

- ✎. Making safety signs;

- ✎. Resources labels;

- ✎. 'How to' cards;

- ✎. Writing instructions, or recording instructions on tape or in photos;

- ✎. Making labelled photos, plans, diagrams and models.

In your science/discovery area

This area of an early years setting is also popular with boys. Finding out how things work, using all their senses, and exploring materials, processes and living things will fascinate them. Older children will be able to get involved in simple experiments, younger ones will just be exploring in a sensory way. Plenty of talking about what happens and how things feel, look, smell, and work, will all prepare children for mark making and recording in writing.

Some **resources** you could include:

- White coats (or shirts), safety goggles and gloves;
- Tubes, funnels, magnifying glasses, bug boxes, tongs and tweezers;
- Trays and other small containers;
- Magnets and objects to experiment with;
- Simple electricity resources such as batteries and bulbs;
- Objects to dismantle, such as clocks, old keyboards, computer pieces, mobile phones, wind up toys, telephones, timers;
- Materials and ingredients for mixing (flour, salt, compost, water, colouring etc);
- Mark making materials, such as clipboards, notepads, labels, whiteboards;
- A desk and pinboard for display.

Reasons for writing:

- Using feely boxes and bags, 'smelling' boxes, treasure baskets;
- Observing living things such as minibeasts, ants, snails, worms or growing things such as seeds, flowers, pips and stones etc;
- Exploring natural objects such as shells, pebbles, cones, seeds, nuts;
- Labelled diagrams, forms, tick sheets, observation schedules;
- Writing instructions, or recording instructions on tape or in photos;

In your woodwork area

If you can manage to provide and equip a simple woodworking area somewhere secluded and easy to supervise, most boys and many girls will be fascinated by the challenge

Some **resources** you could include:

- ✎. A woodwork bench with clamps, to help avoid accidents with saws and hammers;

- ✎. A range of offcuts of different sorts and thicknesses of wood - balsa, softwood, plywood;

- ✎. Chalkboard or large white board for working designs- preferably fixed on a wall;

- ✎. Tool belts - this is a good way to control the numbers in the area;

- ✎. Signing in board for carpenters' names and what they want to make;

- ✎. Child sized, but well made 'real' tools - hammers, small saws, screwdrivers, hand held drills;

- ✎. Sandpaper, measures, rulers, pencils and pens, wood glue;

- ✎. Nails and screws;

- ✎. Relevant books, pictures and posters, plans and drawings.

Reasons for writing:

- ✎. Designing items;

- ✎. Making marks for cutting;

- ✎. Labels for designs;

- ✎. Instructions for making boats, cars, rockets etc.

- ✎. Descriptions with photos;

- ✎. Forms to fill in about resources used;

- ✎. Lists of resources needed for the area when stocks get low;

- ✎. Some simple challenge cards for new or extended designs;

- ✎. Labelled photos, plans, diagrams and models.

Using role play as a stimulus for writing

The idea for role play areas or scenes needs to come from your observations of children's play or from the children themselves. Child-initiated or independent learning time, when you have time to talk with and observe the children will give you a clear insight into their games and the roles they like to take.

Role play stems from the experiences children have at home, in the community and at school. It can also be triggered by film, TV, video and stories. Children use these experiences as starting points for their play and exploration of roles, story lines and events. Adults need to observe and listen carefully to children's interpretations of their experiences, and the way they try to make sense of an often confusing and puzzling world.

A good way to start a new series of role play explorations is to invite a visitor from the community or a local shop, emergency service or other interesting occupation to come to your setting or school. This is also a good way of ensuring that children have role models of males in what can often be a female dominated environment. Brief the visitor before they come, and make sure they can show or demonstrate the importance of both reading and writing in their lives.

The visit can then be discussed with children, deciding what needs to be in the role play area,

what will help them to play the role better. The ideas in the following pages focus on the types of writing and reasons for writing that will be helpful to the play. Some of the ideas will need to be introduced and explained, or demonstrated by an adult in role playing alongside the children and thinking aloud; 'Ahh, I need to write this down' or 'Where is your ticket?' 'Show me your driving license, please sir.'

The setting up of an effective, writing based role play area will engage children in writing signs, making forms, diagrams, pictures, books, lists, letters and many other purposeful writing activities.

For example, making a space rocket will involve planning, drawing, use of scissors, paint and joining materials, making the flight panels and buttons will involve mark making in numbers and letters, even a manual for how to fly the rocket may be needed. You may need to allow plenty of time for making the setting itself, before even suggesting its use for role play or story telling. Don't be tempted to do it all yourself, so it appears like magic overnight or over a weekend. The more the children are involved in devising the area, the more they will feel ownership of the space, and the talking, thinking and wiring together are a huge part of both the fun and the learning. Talk and time will influence the writing that results during the making and the play.

Within a role play scenario, writing should:

- have a purpose which is easy to understand;
- be part of the setting up of the scene as well as the play;
- be initiated by the children rather than an adult;
- be seen as an essential part of children's play;
- make things happen quickly;
- allow children to draw on past experiences;
- have a range of audiences;
- be linked to a challenge or task;
- be modelled by adults in a playful way;
- be fun;
- be valued by adults and other children;
- be extended according to the child's ability and experience;
- link play and real life.

Role Play for Babies and Toddlers

Obviously very young children will not necessarily be so involved in the setting up of an area, and careful observation can lead to changes in the space to maximise the learning. Following children's lead as they begin to play out their experiences will give you a lead when thinking of the resources to provide for first role playing. This may just include fabrics, hats, glasses and shoes. But children soon become interested in the written word and will begin to use little books, pens, and other mark makers to imitate the adult and older children they see.

Role play for the very young needs to be based on the home experiences in houses or shops, but remember to include the resources for both reading and writing that would occur in these familiar situations, whether it is in the kitchen, a baby's room, a toy shop or a hairdresser. The more young children see reading and writing as part of play the more they will have a go themselves when they are ready. Resources could include:

- magazines, newspapers, comics
- TV papers
- forms, letters and cards
- list making pads and pens
- phone books
- catalogues and junk mail.

Try providing two small areas, a kitchen and a food shop, a kitchen and a bedroom, a house and a cafe. This will encourage movement between the two areas, and boys need movement in their play. Remember that outside role play is as important as inside, especially for boys who feel more freedom and become more expressive in a larger space.

Add some photos of children playing and writing in role. This will inspire others to write too.

And join the children as they play, modelling the writing process.

Start small!

14 simple ways to make role play more writing friendly:

✏. Make lots of little blank books and pads from stapled sheets of blank paper and leave them available.

✏. Add a few real pens - fine black felt pens or ballpoints - children love pens!

✏. Offer diaries, appointment books, folders, envelopes etc. for free use in role play.

✏. Put together a basket of writing things - stapler, hole punch, sellotape, paper offcuts, pens and pencils.

✏. Collect some junk mail or forms and add these to the resources.

✏. Sheets of sticky labels for making badges and labels will inspire some children.

✏. Add a jotter by the phone, for messages and numbers.

✏. Buy some small clip boards and white boards and add a pen on a string to each for notes, plans, lists etc.

✏. Make a low level pin board for children's own messages, letters and drawings.

✏. Buy some 'themed' magazines (car magazines, home decor, sports, animals - whatever links with your current theme) and encourage children to read and cut pictures from these for displays, scrap books, posters and little books.

✏. Encourage them to read and write in role by leaving them messages, notes and challenges linked to the theme (an emergency that needs to be attended; an invitation to a party; a job to be done; a broken down car to be mended).

✏. Use a telephone in role to leave messages for other adults or children.

✏. Make a booking for a haircut, a pet injection, a driving lesson.

✏. Join them in the play, modelling writing as you do so.

Who Lives Here?

Make your domestic role play or 'home corner' specific to a job or occupation.

Some ICT opportunities
- talking photo books
- Digital Blue camera
- digital cameras
- computer keyboards
- 'walkie talkies'

Opportunities for writing
- sending and writing messages
- making posters and scrapbooks
- letters, labels
- posters and notices
- badges and signs
- plans, maps and diagrams

Resources
- a domestic play corner or even a bag or basket of resources
- themed crockery and cutlery with animals for a vet, cars for a driving school, fish for a diver's house
- mobile phones, dictaphones, magazines and leaflets
- files, papers, pads, notebooks, diaries, message pads, notice board, 'Post-it' pads, pens, clipboards, calendars and diaries
- materials for making their own specific props for the job they are doing

Ideas for boy friendly settings
- An underwater diving school
- A football club
- A pet shop with unusual pets
- A car showroom
- A fire station
- A spaceship or rocket
- A gym with exercise machines
- A camera or computer shop
- A mobile phone shop
- A pizza parlour with a delivery vehicle
- A camera or photographer's shop
- A superhero home

Spy Command Centre

Spying is a favourite occupation and very high profile with boys. Get them involved in making a Spy Centre to work from. Fill it with gadgets and ICT equipment and watch what happens!

Some ICT opportunities
- talking photo books
- Digital Blue camera
- digital cameras
- computer keyboards
- 'walkie talkies'

Opportunities for writing
- your personal 'spy' details
- mission details
- lists of gadgets needed
- maps and plans
- labelled diagrams
- information on how to operate gadgets
- accident forms
- 'mission accomplished' forms

Resources
- camouflaged area, 'hidey hole' or tent
- gadgets and equipment for spying - magnifying glasses, periscopes, watches, mobile phones, dark glasses, cameras, dictaphones and tape recorders
- files, papers, pads, notebooks, message pads, notice board, 'Post-it' pads, pens, clipboards, calendars and diaries
- maps, plans and diagrams of buildings and areas
- materials for making their own miniature cameras, binoculars

Ideas for challenges and extensions
- 'Apply to be a spy' - adverts, applications and appointments
- Write the details of a new mission.
- Make a list of the gadgets you need.
- Draw a map of the area you are going to spy on. Can you draw an aerial view?
- Make a diagram of how your spy camera works.
- Make a catalogue of all the equipment in your Spy Centre, with photos and descriptions.
- There has been an accident where a spy has been hurt design and fill in an accident form.
- Design a 'mission accomplished' form for spies to fill in.
- Invent a code and write a letter using your code.

Driving Centre

Use boys' love of wheeled toys to inspire writing, making notices, signs, organising driving tests and even writing parking tickets, writing registration numbers, having a car wash.

Some ICT opportunities
- talking photo books
- Digital Blue camera
- digital cameras
- computer keyboards
- 'walkie talkies' and phones

Opportunities for writing
- appointments and tests
- make lists of appointments on clipboard
- clipboard for examiner's notes on tests
- driving test certificates
- driving licences
- information booklets about cars
- car number collections
- recording messages, reminders and note

Resources
- hats, caps, uniforms, badges, overalls, boots
- table or desk, chair and phone
- resources for a car wash - buckets, sponges, water - and clip boards and pens
- tools for fixing and checking cars
- files, papers, pads, notebooks, message pads, notice board, 'Post-it' pads, pens, clipboards,
- phone books, job sheets, booking forms
- materials for making their own notices, labels, registration numbers, parking tickets

Ideas for challenges and extensions
- Organise a system and appointments for driving tests.
- Write the questions for a driving test.
- Make a list of the tools you need to service a car.
- Draw a labelled diagram of how a car works.
- Make a speed camera from recycled materials.
- Phone a car showroom and get some leaflets to make a scrapbook.
- Collect as many car numbers as you can.
- Take photos of all the wheeled toys and cars in your school or setting and make a photo catalogue.
- Make some posters for a Car Wash. Advertise and see who brings their car.

Adventure Camp

Outdoor and adventurous activities make a good focus for both writing and research. Use PE apparatus or outdoor climbing equipment to design and make an assault course for your centre.

Some ICT opportunities
- digital cameras
- Digital Blue camera
- internet research
- computer keyboards
- loudspeakers and phones

Opportunities for writing
- plan an exciting adventure course
- lists of equipment needed
- rules and safety hints
- maps and plans
- labelled diagrams
- adverts and posters
- notices
- badges

Resources
- a base for the planners of the adventure - this could be a pop-up tent
- access to equipment for planning and building adventure equipment
- large sheets of paper, pens, rulers, tape measures and rulers
- supervised access to the internet to research equipment and activity centre information
- materials for making models of assault courses and adventure trails

Ideas for challenges and extensions
- Make leaflets and posters to advertise your adventure camp.
- Draw a big plan of a good assault course. Look on the internet and Google for pictures and information.
- Take some photos of the equipment in your setting or school and use these to make brochures or to add to your plans and diagrams. Can you draw an aerial view?
- Make a list of the rules to keep everyone safe at the Adventure Camp.
- Make a miniature Adventure Camp for superhero models or action figures.
- Draw and label a design for a logo, some badges or a flag for your adventure camp.

TV Master Chef

Being a TV chef will be attractive to some boys, and making real food will be even more exciting. Writing recipes can be good fun if you make them for a special person.

Some ICT opportunities
- Powerpoint presentations
- Digital Blue camera
- Talking photo books
- computer keyboards
- microwave

Opportunities for writing
- writing recipes
- writing simple scripts for TV programmes
- making lists of equipment
- shopping lists for ingredients
- menus
- health and safety rules
- adverts
- labels for containers and ingredients

Resources
- suitable furniture for a kitchen area with cooking equipment
- aprons, hats
- a camera for filming the programme
- clipboards and pens for the producer
- cookery books, recipe cards, menus
- simple real ingredients such as dry pasta, vegetables, flour etc.
- posters and charts
- you could also have a restaurant, take-away or snack bar next to the kitchen

Ideas for challenges and extensions
- Draw a picture of yourself as a chef and make up a name and character.
- Draw a plan of a kitchen that is easy to work in.
- Take turns to be the chef, the TV cameraman and the TV producer and make a film of your cooking programme. Take some photos or film with Digital Blue, and show your programme on Powerpoint or the computer.
- Invent some recipes for story characters such as a giant, Spiderman or Shrek. Draw pictures and make a recipe book.
- Look on the internet for some recipes for children. Print them off and make some. Take photos for your own recipe book of the things you make.

The Builder's Yard

Bob the Builder is a favourite with younger boys. Older ones will like to make a more realistic scenario, so you could take them on a visit to look at a building site or a builder's yard before you start.

Some ICT opportunities
- digital cameras
- photocopier
- mobile phone
- computer
- fax machine

Opportunities for writing
- making plans and drawings
- safety notices and posters
- signs for the site
- lists of supplies
- notices, labels, badges, signs
- checking the equipment
- messages, schedules etc
- letters to suppliers
- signing in board

Resources
- overalls, hard hats, caps
- reflective waistcoats
- reference books on building
- wheelbarrows
- bricks (wooden, plastic or real)
- mud or other 'cement' materials
- maps and plans
- building supply catalogues and leaflets
- tools and tool belts/boxes/kits
- diaries, notes, receipt books
- desk, phones, calculators, computer keyboard, clipboards
- rulers, tapes, trundle wheels
- striped tape and barriers

Ideas for challenges and extensions
- Design and build houses and homes of different sorts - for a giant, a superhero, a troll, a spaceman.
- Look at brick patterns in walls and replicate these with Lego or other bricks.
- Draw labelled diagrams of buildings, machinery or tools.
- Use the Internet to find out about buildings, builders, architecture, tools. make posters or books of what you find.
- Make some safety signs for a building site - what do you need to warn people about?
- Use mud and sticks or bricks to make structures and shelters. Photograph them and make a book.

Superhero Lair

What do superheroes do when they are at home? Do they need to learn to read and write?

Some ICT opportunities
- talking photo books
- Digital Blue camera
- digital cameras
- computer keyboards
- 'walkie talkies'

Opportunities for writing
- labelled diagrams of superhero costumes, kit and special powers
- details of rescues
- lists of equipment needed
- maps and plans
- labelled diagrams of rescues and vehicles
- stories of rescues
- photo story books using superhero models

Resources
- tent, screened area, or home corner screens (painted or covered with fabric)
- phones, computer keyboards, screens
- maps, world map, globe and plans
- costumes, wrist and head bands, gloves
- materials to make superhero kit and equipment
- wheeled toys or boxes to customise into superhero vehicles
- comics, books, superhero figures

Ideas for challenges and extensions
- Make a superhero diary with photos and writing about what the superhero does each day.
- Design and label a costume for a new superhero, complete with their special powers, equipment and vehicles.
- Write or record a message from someone who needs help, and a response from a superhero.
- Make a photo book or powerpoint presentation of a rescue mission, using superhero figures as characters. Write captions for your presentation, then read or show it to your friends or to children in other classes.
- Make menus and shopping lists for superhero foods and drinks. Design colour coordinated meals and drinks.

Once Upon a Time

Choose some story settings that appeal to boys, and they will get involved in the role play and may then be tempted into the writing!

Some stories to use
- Peter Pan or pirate stories
- The Gruffalo
- Puss in Boots
- 3 Billy Goats Gruff
- Jack and the Beanstalk
- The Pied Piper
- The Firebird
- The Snow Queen
- Jason and the Argonauts

Opportunities for writing
- making signs, notices and badges
- rewriting stories and scenes
- captions to pictures and photos
- labelled diagrams
- story maps - what happened and where

Ideas for challenges and extensions
- Make up a new story about existing characters.
- Write a character description of a favourite person from the story.
- Put some familiar characters into a different story - what would happen if the Billy Goats Gruff met Captain Hook? or the Pied Piper rats followed Jack up the Beanstalk? You could make some character cards and story title cards to play story games.
- Use small world characters to make familiar or new stories and record them with a digital camera or movie camera and add a commentary. Show the stories to friends.

Resources
- The resources will be dictated by the story you choose to focus on, but make sure you give lots of freedom for making shelters, labels, messages, notices etc.
- Add cameras, tape recorders or dictaphones so children can record what they do and how their stories develop.

Service or Car Wash Sir?

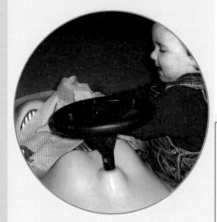

This is an active and possibly quite messy writing activity that even very young boys will enjoy! Offer clipboards and white boards to keep the writing dry.

Some ICT opportunities
- talking photo books
- Digital Blue camera
- digital cameras
- computer keyboards
- 'walkie talkies'

Opportunities for writing
- signs, price lists and labels
- instructions for using the car wash
- petrol prices and signs
- parking and car wash tickets and tokens
- bills and receipts
- checklists for car service
- messages and letters
- shelf labels for the forecourt shop

Resources
- wheeled toys, with number plates and signs
- tools and repair kits
- files, papers, pads, notebooks, diaries, notice board, 'Post-it' pads, pens, clipboards, calendars and diaries
- clip boards and white boards
- duplicate receipt books (or paper with carbon paper between)
- computer and keyboard, phone, message pads
- collection of old car keys
- plastic tubing for petrol pumps

Ideas for challenges and extensions
- Set up a service garage or car wash.
- Talk about how they might make a driving school, with driving instructors, booking lessons, driving tests.
- Draw maps of the area and ways to get to different places.
- Advertise your driving school, car wash or service centre by making posters and leaflets.
- Draw labelled diagrams of how cars work. You could look for some pictures of car engines on the Internet.
- Make a new car catalogue by downloading pictures or asking for leaflets at car showrooms.
- Set up a forecourt shop, a parts department or tyre repair centre.

Down on the Farm

Farms and farming are attractive to some boys. Find out if it is the machinery or the animals that really fires their imagination and customise the setting accordingly.

Some ICT opportunities
- talking photo books
- Digital Blue camera
- digital cameras
- computer keyboards
- mobile phones

Opportunities for writing
- lists of animals, orders for feed and hay
- machinery lists
- labelled diagrams of machinery and how it works
- farming stories about the seasons, the animals, the machinery
- plans and maps of the farm, with crops, buildings, paths and animals

Ideas for challenges and extensions
- Look up some farms on *Google Earth* and see how they look from the air. Make your own aerial views.
- Design a new piece of farm machinery and make a labelled diagram of how it works.
- Write an advert for a tractor driver or farm worker. What will they need to know and be able to do?
- Find and print some pictures of animals or farm machinery from the Internet and make a picture book, machinery catalogue or story.
- Make a seasonal diary of the crops and machinery used for each of the seasons on a farm.
- Find pictures of farm animals and then find out what they eat, where they sleep, what their babies are called.

Resources
- tent, shelter or screens to make an office, farmhouse or farm supply centre
- farm machinery (either child size or small world)
- farm animals, people, builders' trays for soil or compost
- boxes and cartons to make pens, cages and stables
- files, papers, pads, notebooks, diaries, message pads, notice board, 'Post-it' pads, pens, clipboards, calendars and diaries
- pictures of farm machinery and other farming items

Mark making in creative areas

Many boys need opportunities to express themselves through art, and they will find it easier to use larger implements before moving to the smaller ones. Even older boys may find fine motor mark making frustrating and will try to avoid it.

However, this doesn't mean that boys can't put their ideas and perceptions onto paper, making marks that are personal to them. If you make the activity appealing, and encourage work on a larger scale, boys will find it just as engaging as most girls do. It is ideal for developing hand eye co-ordination in preparation for writing, building up muscles in fingers, hands and arms.

Children's natural creativity needs to be valued and celebrated in all forms. Give children frequent opportunities to look at, explore and feel objects before drawing or representing them, give them plenty of choice of how they will work, offer a wide range of equipment, resources and tools, and then accept their interpretations. If you value their marks and accept their meanings, children will be encouraged to express themselves in the ways they choose.

Children often talk as they work, describing what they are doing, the colours they are using and even the story they are drawing or painting. A story often grows and changes as the child talks and draws or paints, and if you listen and watch the creation change you will hear the story, rather than waiting for an end result.

Remember that most boys are interested in action and the events of the present, and many find recap and reflection difficult.

Young children, and particularly many boys, are much more interested in the experience of making a picture or model than they are in talking about it when they have finished. Young children live in the present, and can find discussion and plenary sessions fairly irrelevant to their learning and interests, and so will need plenty of practice in this reflective activity.

Talk about art and artists.

- Boys are often fascinated by abstract art, so recognise and support this interest. Remember that many famous abstract artists are male. Display their pictures and books about the work of such artists as Kandinsky, Picasso, Paul Klee, Jackson Pollock.
- Visit museums and galleries, look at statues, sculptures and other works of art in the community.
- Look at pictures, sculpture and drawings on the internet by putting the names of artists or artistic styles in image or website search engines (try Andy Goldsworthy or Anthony Gormley).
- Put 'snow sculpture' 'wire sculpture' 'wood sculpture' 'recycled sculpture' 'sand sculpture' 'tree sculpture' in Google Images.
- Talk about the arts, encouraging children to develop and express their likes and dislikes, and why they like what the works that they do.
- Invite artists and local people to come to your setting or school to demonstrate their skills, crafts and work. Have a local exhibition with the work of local artists, painters and craftspeople.
- Use the proper terms for tools, equipment and styles of working. If you don't know, use the internet or books to find the answers (or get the Little Book of Painting).
- Remember that creativity is not just about painting and drawing. Try collage, 'junk' modelling, clay, dough, sewing, threading, mobile making, papier mache.
- Offer the widest range of creative materials and tools you can find. Here are just a few:

Materials/media	Surfaces		Tools	
• paint	• paper	• CDs	• fingers, feet	• toothbrushes
• PVA glue	• card	• carpet	• feathers	• rope
• clay	• fabric	• foam	• brushes	• spreaders
• dough	• shower curtains	• plastic trays	• brooms	• string & wool
• papier mache	• plywood	• cartons	• leaves	• kitchen tools
• recycled objects	• stones, slate	• sheets	• cutlery	• sprays
• wire	• leaves, bark	• vinyl sheet	• garlic press	• nuts, cones
• chalk	• newspaper	• fur fabric	• sticks	• scoops
• foam	• plastic sheet	• tarpaulin	• balls	• nails, screws
		• fences & walls		• flowers, seeds

Creative opportunities for babies and toddlers

Babies should be involved in creative and tactile materials as young as possible. Very young babies can be helped to dabble their fingers and toes in sand, paint, gloop and other malleable materials as well as making marks in foods such as tomato sauce, custard and yogurt.

Sitting and crawling babies and toddlers can be offered a wide range of different experiences such as:

- making marks with hands, fingers and toes in trays of soil, coloured rice, flour, cornflour, paint;
- exploring and experimenting with making marks and textures in paints and other substances, using their hands, sticks, brushes, toy cars, bricks to make pathways;
- rolling balls in bowls, paddling pools and on card or paper;
- sitting on paper or card and painting round themselves;
- painting with water or mud on walls and other outside surfaces;
- painting or washing the wheeled toys with bubbly water;
- playing with dough or paper pulp, and shaping it into mounds or lumps;
- using sticks and other tools to make marks in clay or dough;
- using playground chalk on outdoor surfaces;
- sticking and pressing small objects into piles of dough to make sculptures;
- painting on unbreakable mirrors or other shiny, reflective surfaces;
- making handprints and footprints with bubbly water, paint or gloop.

Add texture to surfaces by using 'Hard as Nails' glue to stick on objects such as shells, pebbles, sticks, bark, fabric and recycled objects such as washers, screws, kitchen tools, small toys etc. Or make large scale painting opportunities on big surfaces such as shower curtains, carpet pieces, big sheets of card from boxes.

Secret Water Messages

Painting with water is a magical experience for all children - try using this fascination to encourage mark making too.

Ideas for using water

- Use brooms to make big marks on paths and playgrounds.
- Hang up a shower curtain or big sheets of paper for spraying coloured water.
- Use rollers to draw shapes and pictures on walls and the ground.
- Follow a friend's marks as they lead you round and all over a surface.
- Write your name or words you know in water - how much can you write before it dries? Take some photos of your secret writing.
- Try using a brush in each hand to make big shapes on a flat surface.
- Roll car wheels in water and make tracks on paving or walls.
- Paint words and see if your friends can see what you are writing.
- Draw with chalk and then see if you can follow the patterns and lines with water, erasing them as you go.
- Write secret messages to your friends and see if they can read them before the writing dries. Take a photo of your writing.

What you need

- brushes of all sorts, shapes and sizes
- brooms
- lengths of rope
- sponges, rollers
- squeezy bottles
- small hand sprays
- small buckets or other water containers
- food colouring for colouring water
- washing up liquid to make bubbly water
- walls, fences, blackboards, shower curtains

Mud Patterns

Use very liquid mud mixtures for painting and writing out of doors. Mud washes away more easily than paint - and it's free!

What you need
- brushes of all sorts, shapes and sizes
- brooms
- lengths of rope
- sponges, rollers
- squeezy bottles
- small hand sprays
- small buckets or other mud containers
- mud or earth from a garden or compost from a garden centre
- walls, fences, blackboards, shower curtains, big pieces of card
- a hose for washing surfaces

Ideas for using mud
- Either mix the mid yourself, by adding water - or let the children decide how thick they want it to be.
- Use the runny mud to paint on the ground, on paths or fences and walls.
- Try rollers, sponges, sticks, leaves and other mark makers for different results.
- Pour the mud into shallow containers and use fingers, tools or small world vehicles to make tracks and letters.
- Write huge letters and words on walls and paths.
- Make the mud even runnier and fill plastic squeezy bottles, tomato sauce bottles, or syringes, so the children can make trailing patterns of drips and drops.
- Get some tubing and use this to drizzle runny mud from heights, onto sheets of card or over obstacles, or see if you can direct it into a funnel or container.
- Make circles, spirals and other big patterns on walls or the ground. This will strengthen arm and shoulder muscles for writing.
- Let the children use sponges, a hose or watering can to remove the muddy marks from the ground, walls and other surfaces.

Sticky Pasta

The starch in pasta makes it stick without glue, or if you keep it wet, it can be shaped into letters and words.

Ideas for using cooked pasta

- Cook the pasta until just soft (if you cook it too long it will disintegrate as the children use it). Drain the pasta and rinse well before putting it in shallow trays with a little water.
- Let the children use the pasta to make shapes, patterns and letters on table tops, boards, thick card or plastic.
- If you want the pasta to stick, drain off all the water when the pasta is cooked and use the damp pasta to make the letters and shapes on card or thick paper. Leave them to dry and the starch in the pasta will stick it to the paper without glue. Use this method to make spirals, waves, curves, letters, initials, names and other words.
- Make some coloured pasta by putting cooked spaghetti in a zip lock bag with a few drops of food colouring. Massage the bag gently with your fingers to colour the spaghetti.
- Cover a big table with thick card or plastic sheet and make a collaborative pattern with the spaghetti. Use natural pasta, ready coloured (black is good!) or as many different food colourings as you can find.
- Draw shapes, lines and letters on card and laminate the sheets, or put them in plastic wallets for children to follow with cooked spaghetti.

What you need

- cooked pasta - spaghetti works best for this, but you could use noodles or other pasta shapes
- flat trays of water
- strong paper or card - black or dark colours work well
- white boards
- food colouring (optional)

Letters and Symbols

Offer this activity at festival times, or give the children an opportunity to explore ways of making marks in other cultures and countries.

Ideas for using other lettering and writing systems

- Talk with the children about the signs, symbols and letters from other languages - try to find out what some of them mean. Use the Internet to find symbols, lettering and meanings.
- Put some single symbols on card and laminate them or put them in plastic envelopes so the children can trace over them with water or paint.
- Draw big versions together with water or paint on the ground and walls outside.
- Help the children to make up their own symbols, possibly based on their names, animals, seasons or birthdays.
- Look up some more languages on the internet - use Google Images.
- Explore Celtic symbols and try making some illuminated initials. Google Images 'Celtic letters' has some good examples.
- When you are celebrating Chinese New Year, look together at the symbols for the years and the animals associated with them. Design some new symbols to go with other animals. Write a letter, your name or a badge in a foreign script.

What you need

- brushes, including some Chinese brushes made for writing
- examples of writing from cultures where the characters are different - Chinese, Aztec, Celtic, Japanese, Hindu, Greek, Russian etc
- water or liquid paint
- big sheets of paper or card
- plastic wallets or laminating facilities

Prayer or Message Flags

Prayer flags are traditional in Tibet, Nepal and some other countries. You can make these flags with or without the religious context.

Ideas for making prayer or message flags

- Cut some cotton fabric into shapes - long triangles, strips, small triangles, squares.
- Find some pictures of prayer flags on Google Images 'prayer flags' and look at them with the children. Talk about the way some people use the flags to celebrate festivals, send messages to the gods or to keep them safe on the mountains.
- Talk about the messages and pictures on the flags (click on some of the Google pictures to find out more).
- Offer the children fabric, paints and brushes to make their own flags with messages and pictures on them.
- Put your flags up on sticks and canes or on longer pieces of string. Look at the Google pictures to see how. Make sure you put them where the wind can catch them and help to convey the messages.
- Make some message bunting from a long piece of string or a washing line with triangular flags, each with a child's name on it.
- Work together to make a class or group flag with all the children's names on it and a picture or symbol for the whole group. Hang your flag up outside your room.

What you need

- brushes of all sorts, shapes and sizes
- paints
- pieces of fabric, cut in strips, triangles and squares (cotton works best)
- canes or sticks
- string
- cable ties (optional)
- somewhere out of doors to put the flags

More Mark Making

Children love making marks with all sorts of objects and mark makers. Try some of these to strengthen wrists, fingers and hands for holding pencils and pens.

Ideas for using unusual mark makers

- Offer a range of mark makers, so children can experiment and explore them freely.
- Put big sheets of paper on the ground (lining paper or ends of wallpaper are good).
- Make tracks and lines with cars, tyres, rollers, shoes, on long pieces of paper.
- Pin paper on a fence for mark making with sponges, brushes, fruit nets and other softer markers.
- Ride on bikes and even a skateboard through a shallow tray of paint and along paper or a path.
- Line a paddling pool with paper and work together to manipulate paint-covered balls around on the bottom of the pool.
- Use tweezers and ping pong balls, or tongs and bigger balls - dip the balls in paint and drop them onto flat or sloping pieces of paper.
- Sit in the middle of a big piece of paper and draw a pattern round yourself with painty chain or rope.
- Use different colours of paint to match car colours and make coloured tracks. What happens when different coloured cars meet and their tracks merge?
- Use newspaper and see if you can completely cover the writing with tyre tracks or prints of objects.

Try some of these

- feathers
- sticks, logs and twigs
- lengths of rope or chain
- kitchen implements such as mops, fish slices, wooden spoons, brushes
- the nets from fruit and vegetables, on their own or filled with sponge or tissues
- small world vehicles
- animals
- construction toys such as Lego, Mobilo, Stickle Bricks
- shoes, wellingtons, gloves
- bubble wrap, plasticine, clay

You've Been Framed!

Portraits are another way of linking pictures and letters. Make some simple frames and give children the chance to paint each other or even do self portraits.

Ideas for using picture frames for protraits

- Hang up some of the picture frames on walls, fences or other surfaces (you can even put them flat on the ground for a different sort of experience). If you put some paper under the frame, children can keep their work when it is done.
- Talk with the children about portraits and self-portraits. You could use Google Images 'self portrait' or 'portrait child'.
- Offer the children brushes and paint or chalk to make portraits of each other or self portraits of themselves.
- The children could put a name label on their portrait frame and then use the digital camera to take permanent pictures of their work.
- Use the frames for notices and announcements - 'Wanted' posters, 'lost' and 'found' notices, adverts etc.
- Hang an unbreakable mirror up and let children paint their own reflections. Record these in photos.
- Line picture frames with foil for different self-portraits.
- Use frames on blackboard surfaces for notices, signs and announcements by adults and children.
- Back a bog frame with cork for a notice board and hang low down so children can pin up their own writing, pictures, cuttings, poems etc.

What you need

- brushes and paints
- chalks
- old picture frames
- digital camera
- unbreakable mirrors or silver foil (optional)

Mark making in small world

Small world play helps imagination _and_ manipulation!

Small worlds fascinate most children, who find them a real outlet for creativity and role play in miniature. Both boys and girls enjoy farm, circus and zoo play with animals, although girls will may enjoy using people in such play, boys may favour machinery, structures and objects. Story scenes are also popular - superheroes, TV characters, action figures, and dolls such as Barbie and Action Man all give children opportunities to develop their imaginations while using fingers and hands to manipulate and operate the toys, their equipment and clothing.

- As many boys do not develop their fine motor skills as early as girls, it can be difficult for them to play with small world scenes with small pieces and fiddly characters. Using large trays or boxes will ensure more access for boys.

- Remember that you can put small world scenarios in the outside area. A farmyard or small world digger site in the grass and earth is much easier to set up outside than inside, and looks more realistic.

- Make sure children can find the small pieces of card, paper and supports they need to make notices, signs, labels and instructions to go with their creations.

- Adding bricks, construction toys and found materials also expand the opportunities for extending layouts, changing levels and making roadways.

- Larger items such as telephones, books and message boards increase the scope of play with small world scenes. Small world play is a miniaturised version of role-play, and many small world scenarios can be created from full body play, expanding children's understanding of what characters may be doing or saying.

- As with all play, children need to see adults playing, talking and writing in small worlds, and small world play can lead to a wider vocabulary and talk before writing. Small world play can encourage boys to concentrate and focus, as long as it is made appealing to their interests.

The ideas on the following pages can be used with children of all ages.

Swamped!

Playing with gloop, slime, foam and other sensory materials are all good ways to engage boys in developing fine motor skills, almost without noticing what they are doing.

Ideas for using sensory materials

- Offer the children these sensory materials for free play before expecting them to become creative and imaginative.
- Provide a range of small world collections in baskets or a small trolley, so the children can choose when to incorporate them and whether to have animals, underwater creatures, people or nothing.
- As they explore the materials talk with them about the texture and behaviour of different substances. Encourage them to use their hands and fingers to make marks, piles, trails and prints. Some children may naturally start to make letters and words or draw pictures, others will just enjoy the sensory experiences they offer.
- As children get more experienced with the materials, try leaving a small world animal or person to start off a story. Older children may enjoy a challenge, such as 'Can you make a shelter in the foam for this lost explorer?' or 'Can you make a raft for these shipwrecked sailors?' or 'This blue water is the ocean. Can you make an ocean scene?'
- A challenge for older children - 'The monsters are angry because the people keep falling in their favourite mud holes and frightening the frogs they like to eat. Help the monsters stop people from falling in when the monsters are not there to scare the people away.'

What you need

- shallow trays
- one of these mixtures
  gloop (cornflour and water)
  slime (soap flakes and water)
  shaving foam
  finger paint
  soft dough
  lots of dried beans or lentils
  dry flour
  chopped jelly
  cooked pasta
- sticks, stones, pebbles, shells, nuts, dry pasta
- food colouring or ready mix paint (optional)
- small world animals, vehicles and people

Traffic Jam

Road mats and small world cars give children another way to explore the world through play. There are also lots of reasons for writing if the play is encouraged to develop by giving plenty of uninterrupted time.

What you need
- road mats
- baskets of
  cars and trucks
  planes and airport vehicles
  small world people
  emergency vehicles including
    helicopters
  space vehicles
  safari or zoo jeeps and trucks
- pens, card, scissors, stickers
  for making notices and labels

Ideas for using road mats
- Commercial road mats can be too small for extended play, so you could make your own on a carpet offcut, using paint or markers. Or you could give the children a plain piece of carpet and playground chalk to draw their own maps and layouts.
- Use Google Earth to look a some towns from the air, so children get to know about aerial views and maps.
- Give the children plenty of time and space to play freely with the roadways, vehicles and objects in their own way.
- As children get more experienced with this sort of play, you can begin to drop in some suggestions or challenges, playing alongside them and saying such things as;
  'Oh dear, my car has broken down. I hope no-one bumps into it! Who can help me?' or
  'There's a really big traffic jam/fire/accident in the town, we need the police to sort it out.' or
  'A plane has crashed on the runway and the people need to be rescued, because some of them are hurt!' or
  'A kitten is stuck up a tree, who can rescue it?'
- You could also model or suggest using notices, signs, diversions, road blocks etc. If you provide a small basket of card, pens, scissors and tape, they can make their own signs and stick them to bricks or fences.

Buried Treasures!

Use your sand tray, a builder's tray or a washing up bowl to encourage reading and writing in small world imaginative play.

What you need

- containers for sand (several trays would be useful so children can work on different ideas at the same time)
- objects to bury
  shiny tiny 'treasures'
  fake jewels, sequins, beads, foreign coins
  plastic letters and numbers
  puzzle pieces (dry sand only!)
  shells
  glass beads
- sticks, card, scissors, pens
- tweezers, small brushes, magnifying glasses

Ideas for making treasure hunts and games in sand

- Burying and finding is a good support to concentrating and focusing, so do plenty of simple hiding and finding with small objects such as small world figures, plastic bugs, stones and pebbles, before moving on to challenges.
- Once children are familiar with the systematic 'hide and find' of treasure hunts, you can start to challenge their thinking by hiding things with clues and challenges:

'There are 25 coins hidden in the sand. Can you find all of them in five minutes?'

'There are some letters hidden in the sand, can you find the letters of your name?'

'Here is the pirate's treasure chest, dig up the treasure and fill the chest.'

'Can you find all the puzzle pieces and make the puzzle?'

'Here is a string. Can you find some beads to make a necklace with a pattern of red/white/red/white beads?'

'Now can you make your own necklace pattern and write the pattern on a card as a challenge for your friend?'

'Bury these treasures in the sand and draw a treasure map to show your friends where to find them.'

'Here are some clues to find the treasure in the sand. Can you work out where it is? Were you right?'

'Now can you make your own treasure clues?'

Mark making out of doors

'Being outdoors has a positive impact on children's sense of well-being and helps all aspects of children's development. Being outdoors offers opportunities for doing things in different ways and on different scales than when indoors. It gives children first-hand contact with weather, seasons and the natural world. Outdoor environments offer children freedom to explore, use their senses, and be physically active and exuberant.'

Early Years Foundation Stage; DCSF 2007

Generally young boys prefer to be playing outside, they enjoy the space for running and a less restrictive atmosphere, where sound making and sudden movement are tolerated! They have a need to move and explore so it is very important to plan for and provide opportunities for writing that engage them. It is important that boys do not see writing just as an indoor activity, and the bags and boxes suggested here are just a few that are likely to appeal to many boys. However, you need to observe and listen to the children you work with in order to develop resources that will inspire them and their unique set of interests.

The adults in your setting or school need to get outside and model using writing in their play too, there is no reason why a story or poem or song cannot be seen to be composed, written and told outside. Get involved in the roles that outside writing boxes and bags present, and make sure you value writing that is done outside as much as writing done indoors.

Boys like to use tool boxes and tool belts, so kit these up with writing tools and paper, card, tape, scissors etc. for the children to take and use outside as they play.

Many of the outdoor boxes or bags suggested are just as relevant for younger children. As in the small world ideas, these may not involve as much writing at a younger age, but will create language and vocabulary and muscle development.

One simple way to involve regular writing is to have a signing out system for outdoor resources. This also means that other children know where the things are if they want to play too, naturally combining reading and writing. You could also have a laminated sheet and dry wipe pen for children's suggestions for other resources they need, or when resources are broken or need replacing.

When I'm Cleaning Windows!

Another opportunity to work with water, brushes and buckets, as well as clipboards and other writing tools.

Ideas for window cleaners
- Offer the window cleaners' box as part of free play resources and don't try to influence the free use to start with.
- Show the children how to use the tools and equipment, how a squeegee works, how important it is to use clean water and not too many bubbles.
- Encourage them to 'wash' the windows of buildings, play houses, vehicles, painted doors.
- Offer the children clip boards and pens to write receipts, and money belts to collect the payments.
- As children get more experienced with the materials, you could suggest that they invent a name for their window cleaning business and some badges, bills and notes for customers.
- They could also make some signs for their vehicle and put up adverts for their services.

What you need
- bowls and buckets
- plastic tool boxes or tool tidies
- cloths, dusters
- squeegees, window scrapers
- plant sprayers
- water and non-allergenic washing up liquid
- caps and overalls
- low, safe steps or stools

Come Exploring

Explorers and exploration are interesting to many boys, particularly if you can provide lots of equipment and gadgets to hang from belts and pockets of jackets.

What you need
- tents or shelters
- camouflage or safari jackets, waistcoats and hats (get these from army surplus stores or markets)
- binoculars, cameras, water bottles, compasses, phones
- backpacks
- magnifying glasses
- metal detectors
- sleeping bags and camp fire materials (fake!)
- maps, notebooks, reference books of plants, animals, insects, birds

Ideas for explorers
- Talk with the children about what explorers need and what should be in their backpacks. This will give children lots of ideas for play with a purpose.
- Hang the explorers' bags on hooks near your outdoor area, where children can take them and return them easily.
- Set up some tents and shelters so there is a base for the play, and join in, as long as you don't constrain their exploration and imagination.
- You could make a safari vehicle from chairs covered with fabric or disguised by a big box painted with camouflage.
- Look at maps together to decide where you will go to explore and collect things.
- As children get more involved in the play, try making some comments and suggestions, such as:
  'We could be bird spotters today - let's look for an eagle.'
  'Shall we be archaeologists? We could look for buried treasure or caves.'
  'Can I come with you? Where are you going? Can you show me on the map?'
- Model making maps, lists and plans. Draw diagrams of your camp sites and the places you have been, animals you have seen or rescued.
- Write postcards, letters and reports to send home.

Emergency!

Rescuing people is something superheroes do, so many boys will enjoy the opportunity to rescue people in 'real life' play situations.

Ideas for emergency workers

- Get as many different backpacks as you can manage, so you can equip each for a different service. You could put a tape cross for ambulance bags, a red band for firefighters, and a police helmet badge for police bags. Children can use suitably customised bikes and other wheeled vehicles.
- Make sure each bag has writing implements, notebooks, clipboards etc. so the children can write in role, taking names and details of the accidents and emergencies.
- Help the children to take photos, draw plans make lists and diagrams.
- Use books and the Internet to find out about the jobs emergency workers do. You could ask some to visit, making sure they remember to mention the writing they do, and perhaps bringing examples.
- Make badges and signs. Get some striped 'crime scene' tape to keep spectators away.
- Add some equipment for a hospital, so injured people can get treatment from doctors and nurses. Give them a bag too, with stethoscope, hypodermics and medicines.
- Older children may like to have a set of 'Emergency Scene' cards with different situations for them to sort out.
- Make identity badges using digital photos and a laminator, and put these in conference lapel badge holders.

What you need

- backpacks
- medical kit for ambulance men or paramedics - first aid kits, bandages, hats and badges - and even a stretcher
- firefighter kits with hats, hose, badges, goggles, walkie-talkies
- police hats, phones, badges, flashing lights, handcuffs, notebooks, torches
- you could make some simple tabards in key colours, and even some tool or kit belts with hooks and pockets for equipment and tools

Superheroes Rule Outside!

This bag is likely to be very popular and children will need plenty of time to use the objects actively before introducing or modelling any writing activities!

What you need
- capes, armbands, wristbands
- masks and head bands
- phones, gadgets and special objects for 'powers'
- special writing implements - pens that light up, red painted clipboards etc.

Ideas for superhero play
- Give plenty of free play time when you introduce these resources, some children will never tire of the active, physical elements of the play, so you may need to be available to:
    - listen to their stories after the play;
    - act as a scribe to write these down;
    - start off the stories;
    - give leadership in new situations;
    - help them to manage the play.
- Some children may get involved in writing or drawing the superheroes, or may become the photographer, taking photos of the play so you can make a book or powerpoint presentation for the whole class to see.
- Older children may enjoy making up new superheroes, describing and demonstrating their powers and making up new adventures for them.
- If you play alongside, you could suggest making a new superhero car or plane, a labelled diagram of his or her lair, or some information about his or her mortal enemies who are trying to stop the rescues.

Roll, Bounce and Catch!

This bag will give children lots of fine motor practice in hand-eye coordination. It's also a lot of fun.

Ideas for fine motor skills

- These bags may need some adult introduction and support to play and invent games for individuals and small groups. Sit and look at the contents together and talk about how they could be used in games and activities.
- Play some of the games together, encouraging the children to make up the rules and scoring systems.
- Show the children lots of different ways of using the equipment - rolling, carrying, balancing, tossing, passing with balls and bean bags, and numbering buckets, boxes, skittles and circles to make different scores.
- Help the children to make circles, scoring lines, start and finishing lines with chalk, and model how to be the scorer, with a clipboard and pen.
- As children get more used to making up their own games, you can help them by writing down their rules and instructions, then reading them back as they play the games again.
- Older children could use the Internet to find more games to play, or they could photograph their games to make a book of games for the class to play, complete with equipment lists, rules and scores.
- Plan and arrange a sports day or competition, making lists, planning the games and races, recording the scores.

What you need

- one or more backpacks
- a selection of
  balls
  bats
  bean bags
  skittles
  skipping ropes
  playground dice
- playground chalk
- clipboards or white boards and pens
- certificates and rosettes for winners

Twelve Key Tips for engaging boys in writing

These twelve key factors in supporting the writing activity of young boys appear to be crucial. You may think of more as you continue to engage boys in an activity which our culture values highly as a key to future success in learning.

1. Many boys learn best out of doors, where there is space and they can work on a larger scale. Offer plenty of opportunities to write out of doors.

I have a dead scorpion.

2. Most boys will be more likely to write if they are in role. Offer plenty of opportunities for writing in role play areas and in costume.

3. Boys often write on the move. They will write standing up, kneeling on a chair, resting on a shelf, even lying down. Make sure that writing on the move is possible and has your approval.

It is brilliant and all cos the colour is best.

4. Because boys often develop fine motor skills later than girls, they need more space and like to work on a larger scale than many girls. Offer all children a choice of where, what and how they write, by providing different sizes and scales of materials and places to work.

The stinger is grey too as well don't forget the stinger.
Hi Hi.

5. Writing with real resources and materials, such as pens, notebooks, clipboards etc. gives purpose to many boys' writing. Collect as many real life writing resources as you can find.

6. Unusual surfaces and mark makers, such as decorators' brushes, pieces of wood, plastic sheets, white boards etc - may inspire some boys to write and make marks. Offer the widest range of mark makers and surfaces that you can think of, and value all methods and means of communication equally.

'Some boys who are at risk of becoming disaffected at a very young age have shown significant improvements if their learning takes place outside. Opportunities which reflect all six areas of learning outdoors must be available.'

Helen Bilton; Learning Out of Doors; David Fulton; 2005

7. Boys will often be inspired to write for real purposes, and are less likely to write to please adults or for routine purposes. Make plenty of opportunities for purposeful writing.

8. Models of adults as writers (and particularly models of older boys and men) will inspire many boys to write. When you invite visitors into your school or setting, enlist their help in modelling writing as a real and male activity.

9. Having a sympathetic audience for their writing is vital for self esteem and motivation. Listen, respond and give appropriate praise when boys show or read their writing to you.

10. Boys will often write more briefly, but more succinctly than girls. Offer different ways of approaching writing activities - lists, labelled diagrams, maps and plans - as well as running text. Boys may favour these other ways of expressing their ideas and experiences.

11. Boys' writing often springs from their interests, and this can provide you with a way to stimulate interest in writing. Make sure you observe and listen to boys as they play and talk, so you are in tune with their interests.

12. Boys often choose activities that are not accompanied by adults. Make sure you monitor what boys choose to do, what they are interested in and who they are playing and working with. Add inspiring writing materials to the activities that attract boys, and join these activities to model their use.

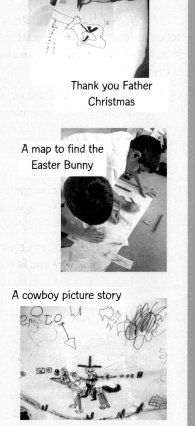

Thank you Father Christmas

A map to find the Easter Bunny

A cowboy picture story

'The types of play that boys and girls engage in is enhanced or diminished by the quality of the learning environment inside and out. Practitioners must take responsibility for ensuring the learning environment is planned to inspire, challenge and intrigue every child. However, sometimes practitioners find the chosen play of boys more difficult to understand and value than that of girls. They may choose activities in which adults involve themselves least, or play that involves more action and greater use of the available space, especially outdoors.'

Confident, capable and creative: supporting boys' achievements; DCSF Primary National Strategy; 2007

Bibliography

Biddulph, Steve	Raising Boys	Thorson (1997)
Bilton, Helen	Learning Outdoors	David Fulton (2005)
DfES	The Early Years Foundation Stage	DfES (2007)
DCSF	Raising Boys' Achievements in Writing	DfES (2004)
DCSF	Improving Boys' Writing	DSCF (2005)
DCSF	Confident, Capable and Creative: Supporting Boys' Achievements	DSCF (2007)
DCSF	Boys' Writing (flyers)	DSCF (2005)
Fisher, Robert	Boys into Writing	David Fulton (2002)
Gurian, Michael	Boys and Girls Learn Differently	Jossey Bass (1999)
Gussin Paley, Vivian	Boys and Girls, Superheroes in the Doll Corner	University of Chicago (1986)
Hall, N and Robinson A	Exploring Writing and Play in the Early Years	David Fulton (2003)
QCA	Can do Better	QCA (1998)
West, P	What is the Matter with Boys?	Choice Books (2002)
Wolfendale, S and Bryans, T	Word Play	David Fulton (2006)
Bayley, Ros and Featherstone, Sally	Boys and Girls Come Out to Play	Featherstone Education (2005)
Various Authors	The Little Books (Writing, Messy Play, Outdoor Play, Small World, Mark Making)	Featherstone Education

websites and research

Australian Broadcasting Corp http://www.abc.net.au

The Getting it Right Enquiry 2002 Australia http://www.cis.org.au and search for 'Getting it Right'

Bauer Gabrielle; 2005; Why Boys Must Be Boys; Canadian Living http://www.readersdigest.ca/mag/2002/05/boys.html

Doran P; Boys can do better; 2003; Kent County Council www.nationalliteracytrust.org.uk/database/boys/Kentcasestudies.pdf

Holden Cathie; 2002; Contributing to the debate: the perspectives of children on gender, achievement and literacy Journal of Educational Enquiry, Vol. 3, No. 1, 97

Teachers' TV March 2007-02-26 Video

Stevens Kathy 2006 Gender Differences Impact Learning and Post—School Success on the Council for Exceptional Children website www.cec.sped.org

www.literacytrust.org.uk website of the National Literacy Trust, includes research, resources, initiatives and links to other organisations.